Vol 4

# MAZE

Ages 4-6

# FOR KIDS

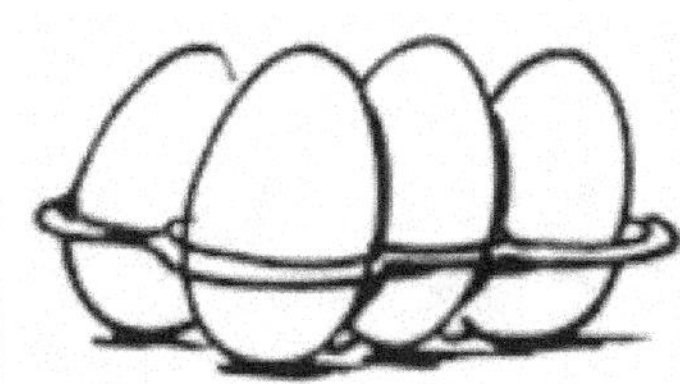

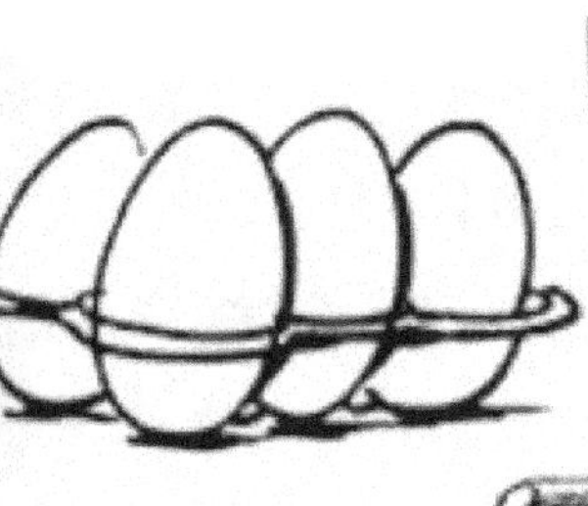

# MAZE BOOK

## SOCIAL MEDIA

 /MySweetBooks1

 /MySweetBooks1

 /MySweetBooks1

 /MySweetBooks

Email Us : mysweetbooks1@gmail.com

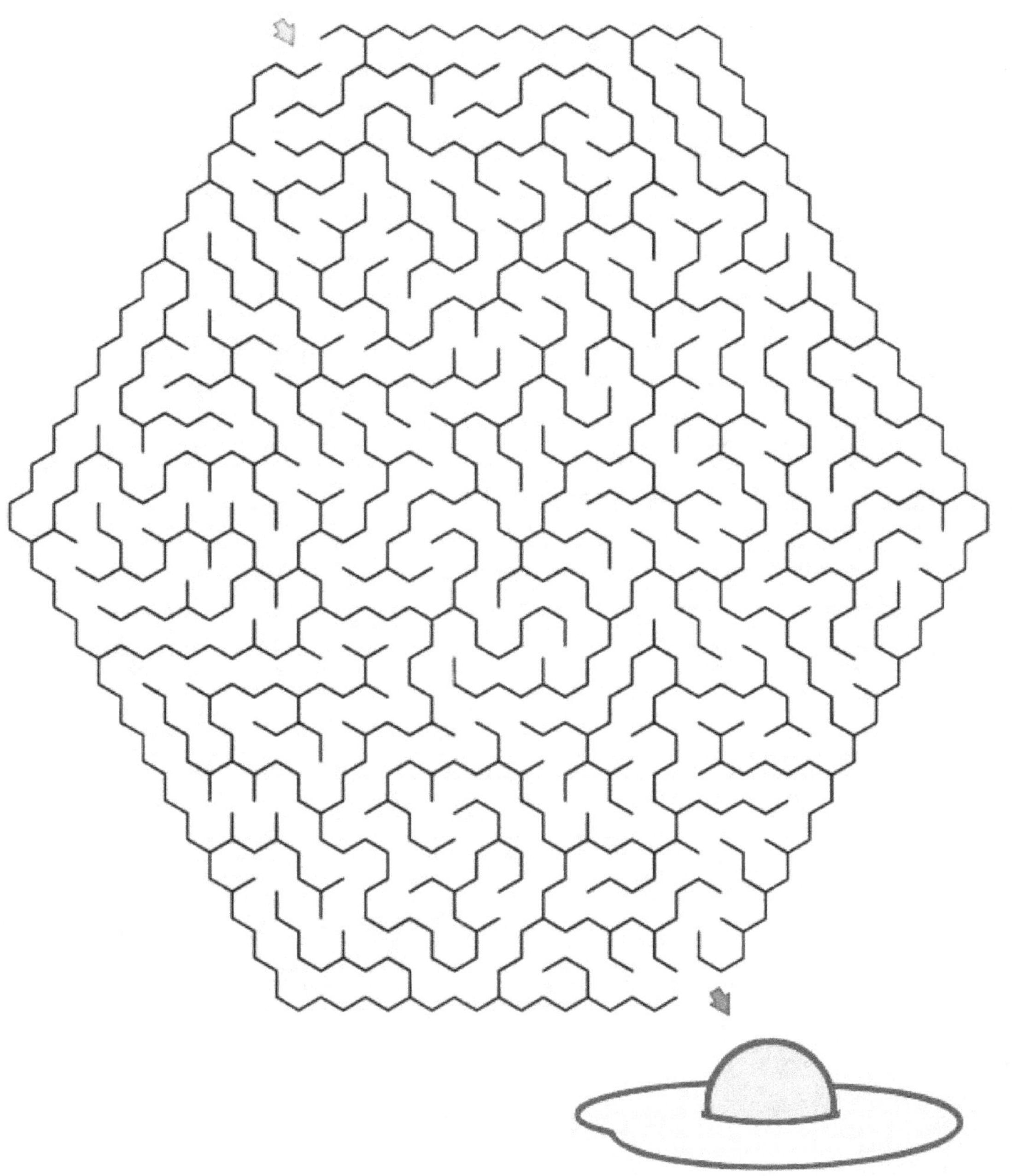

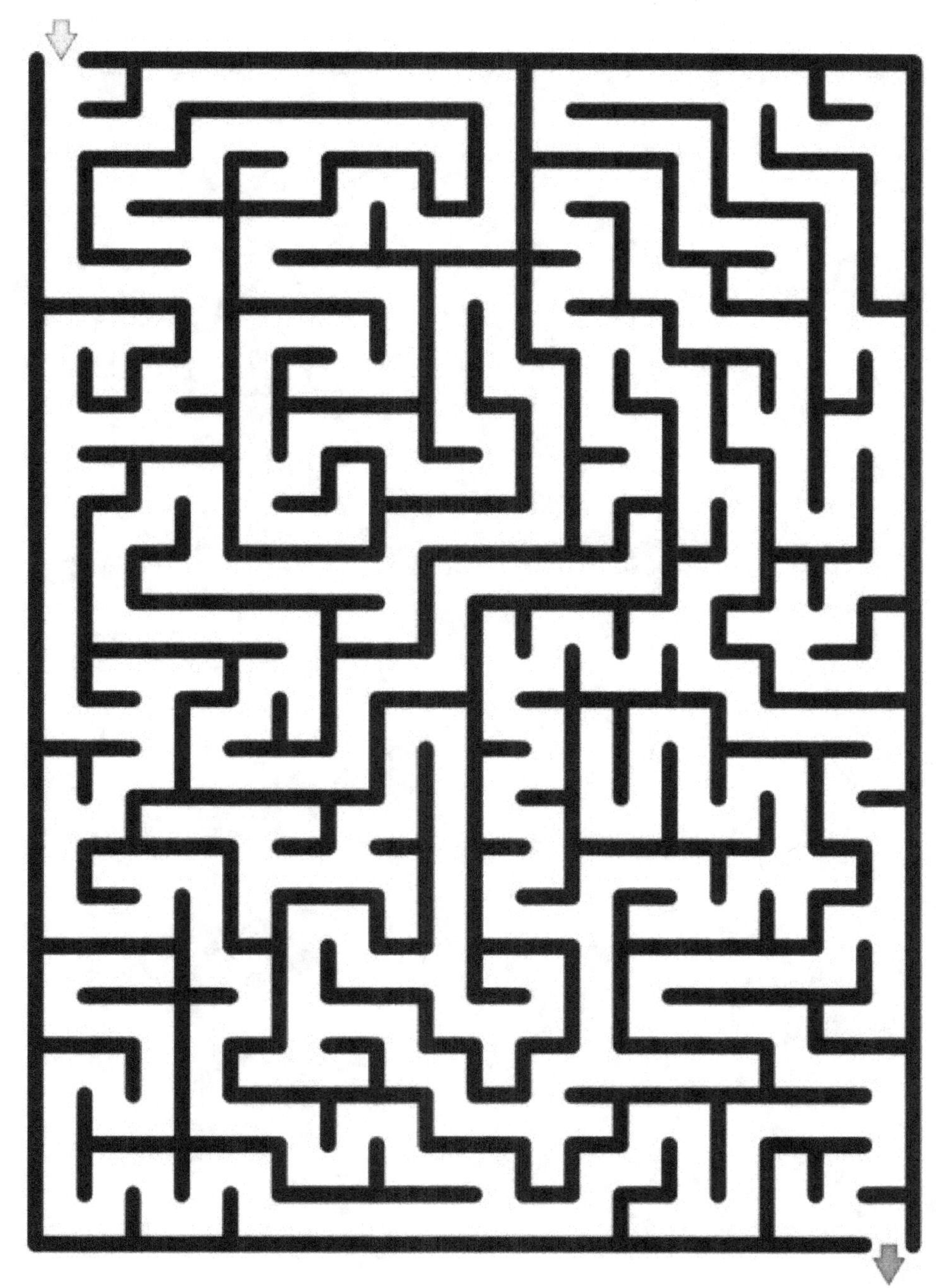

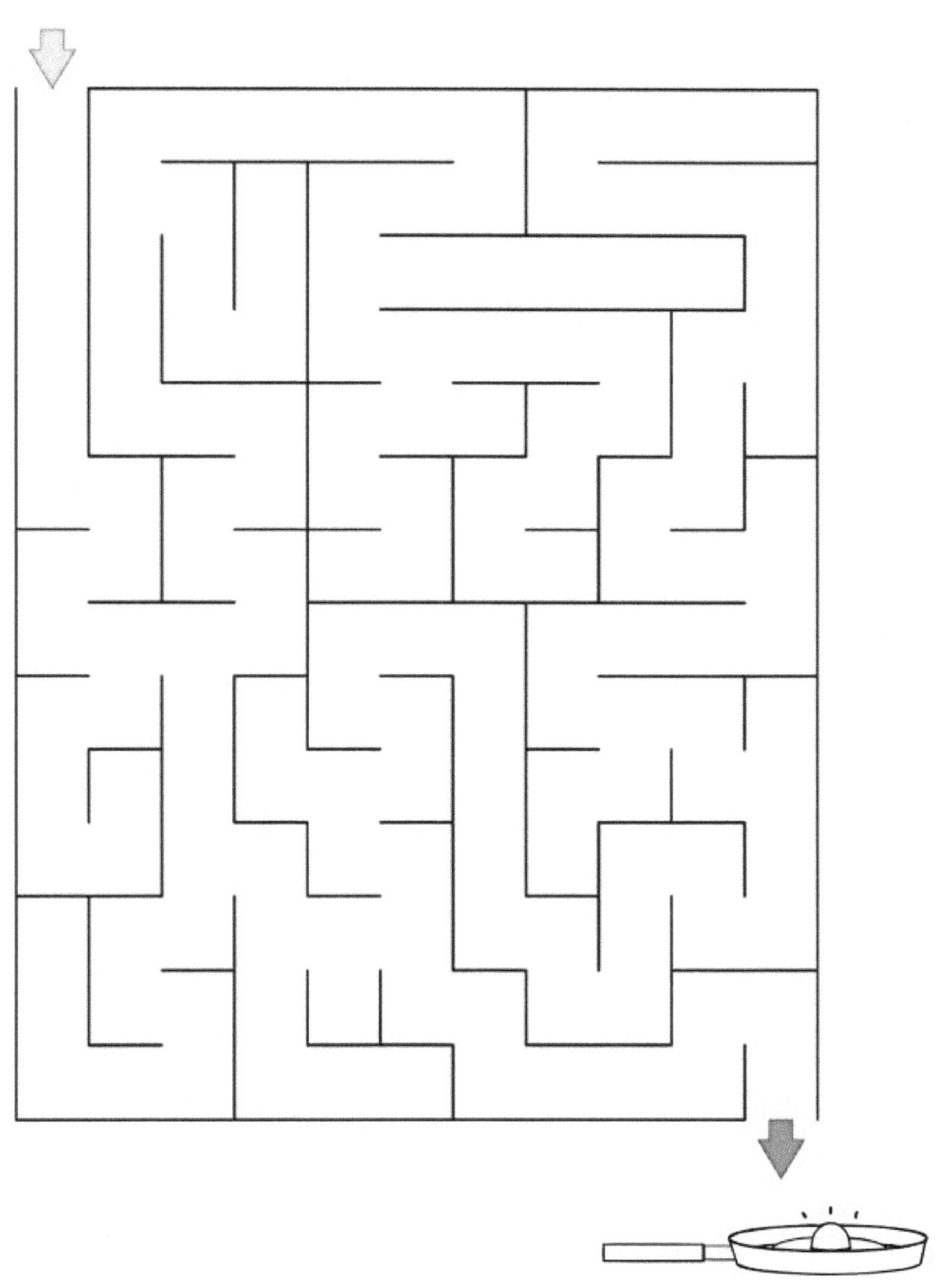

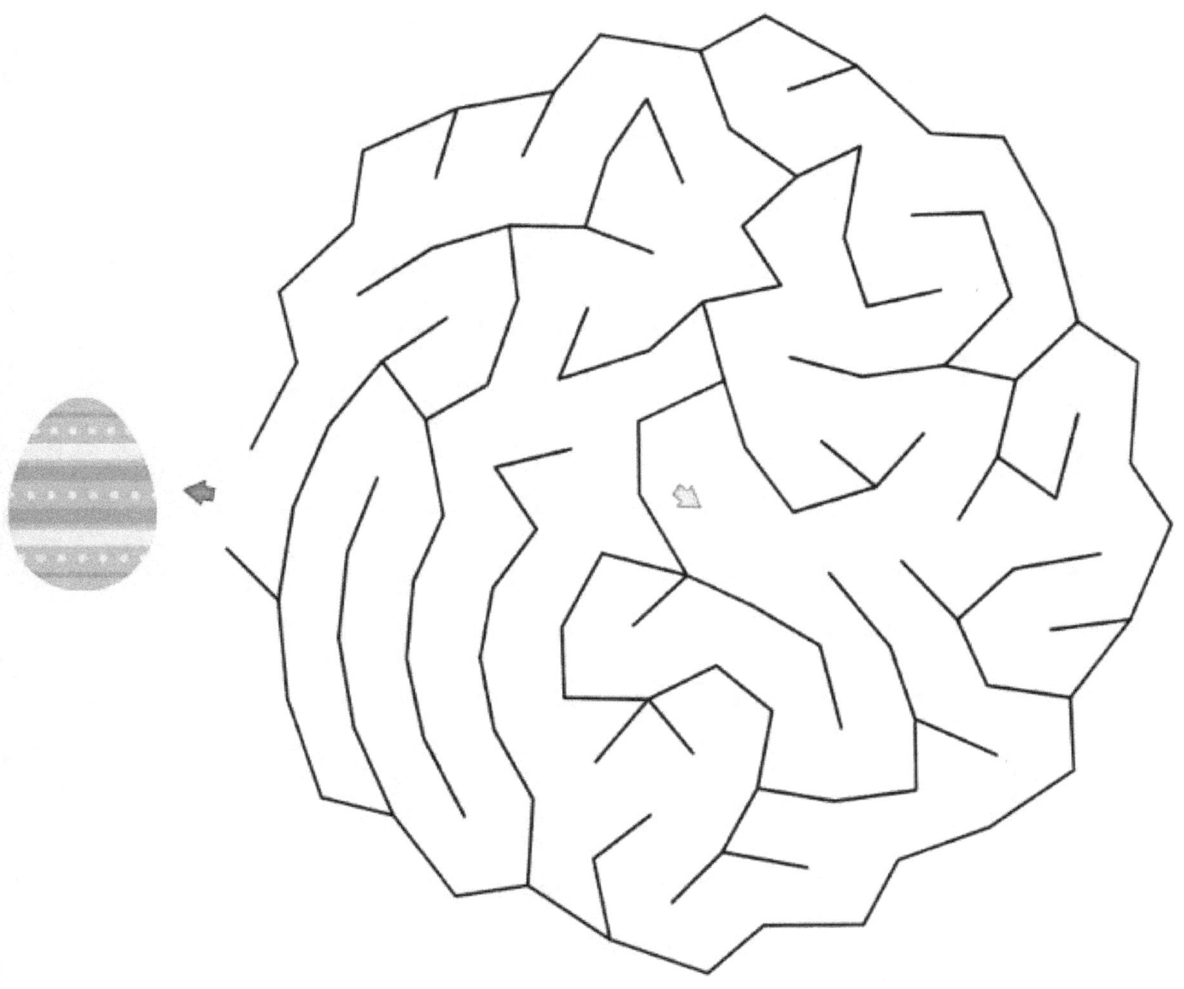

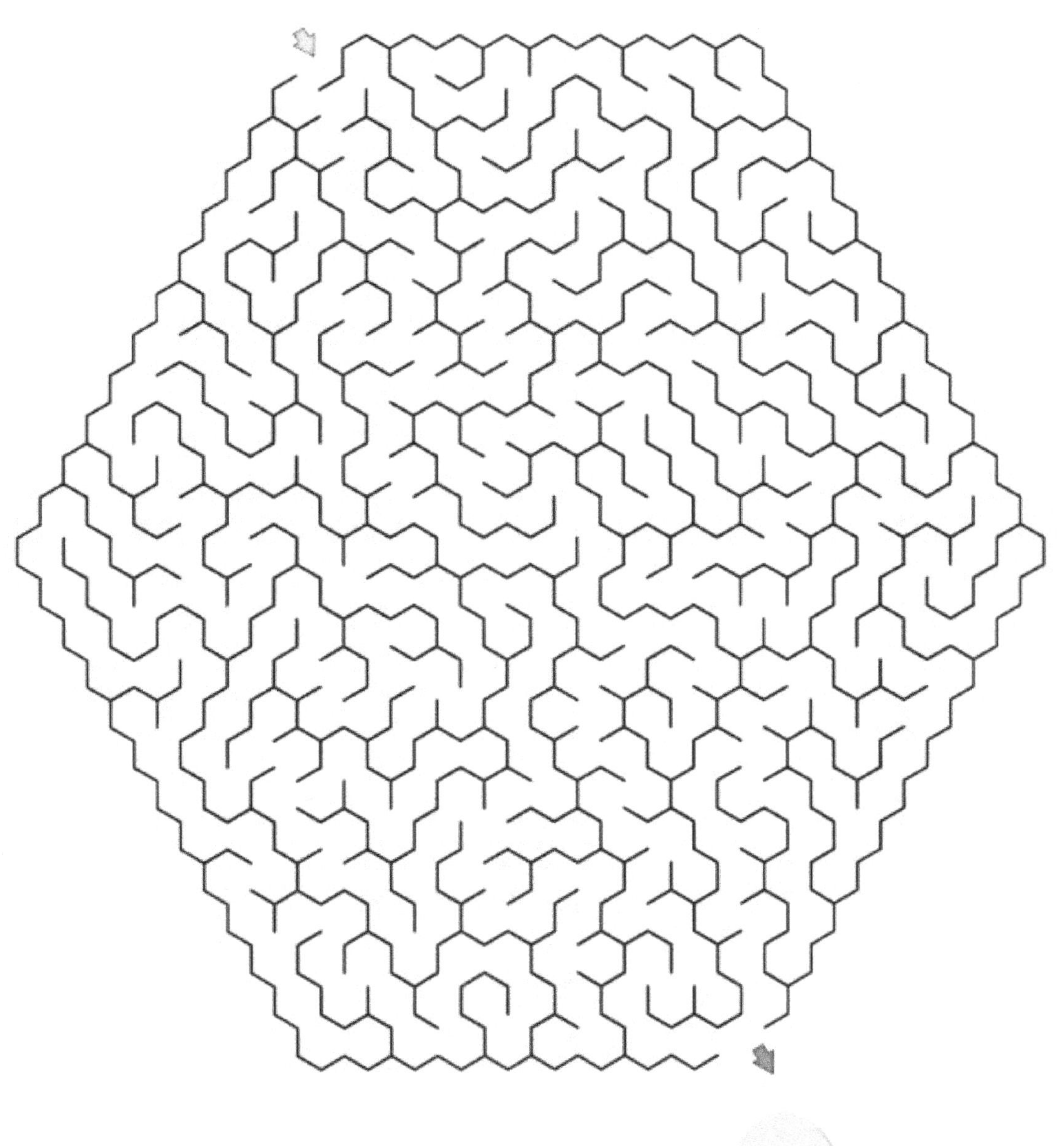

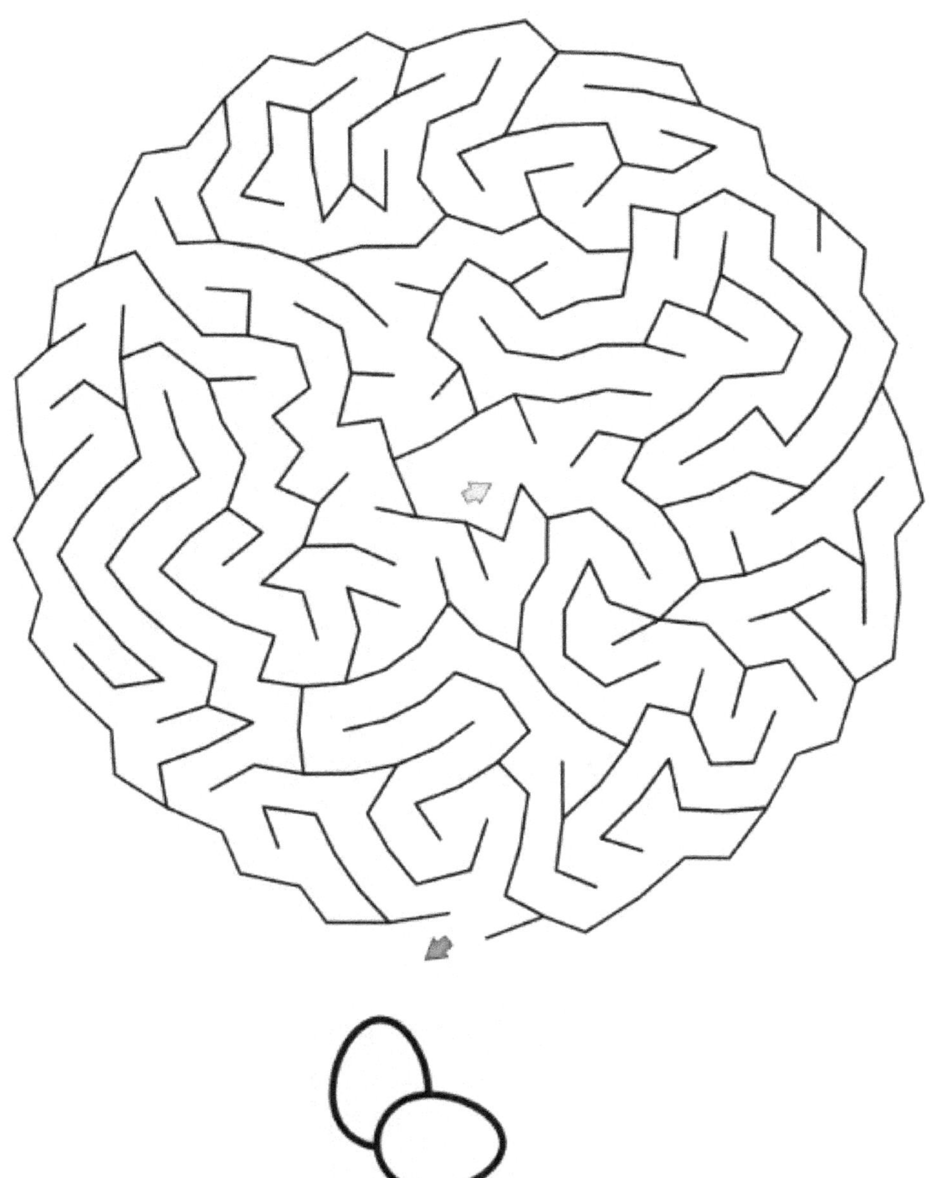

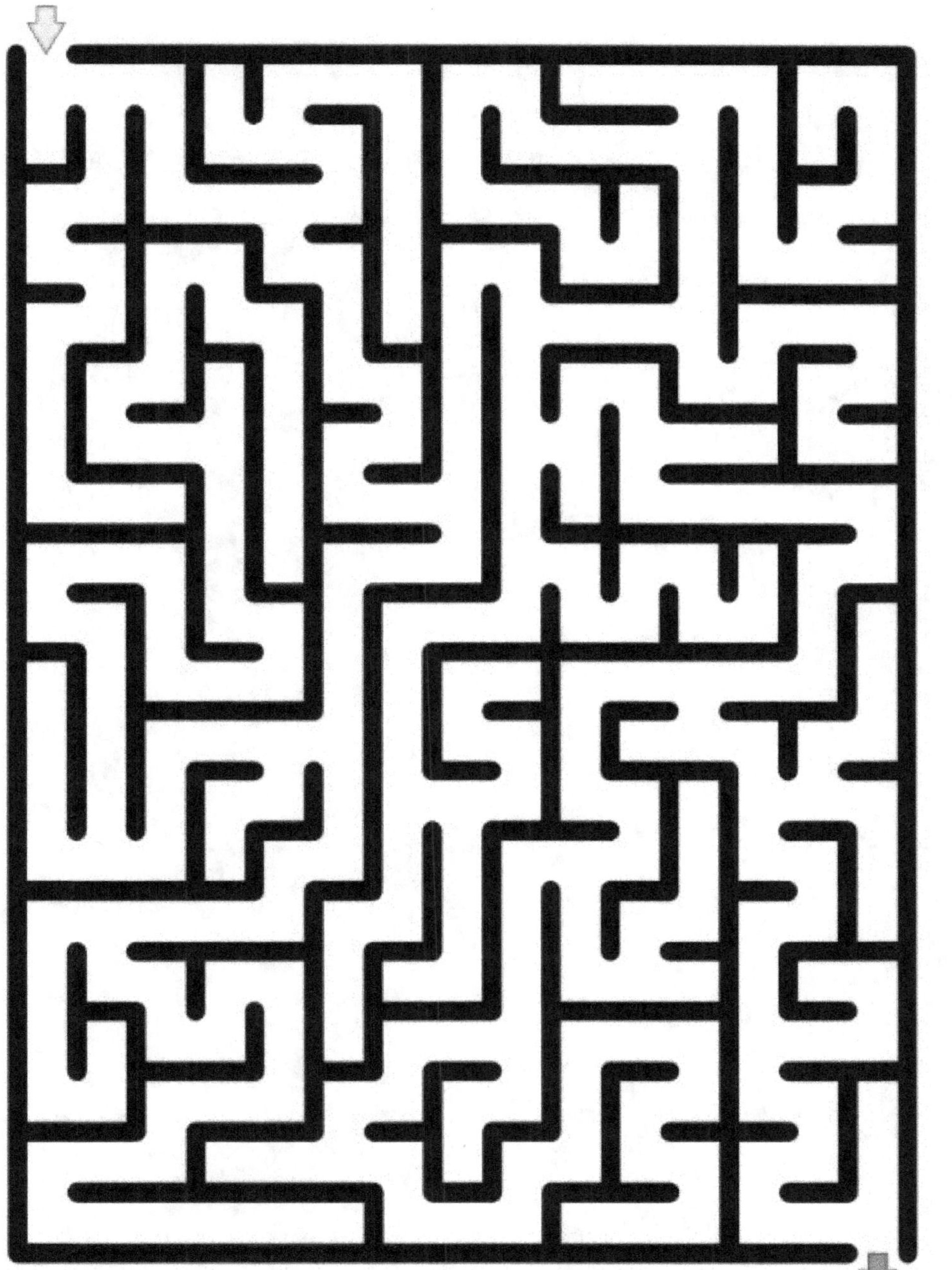

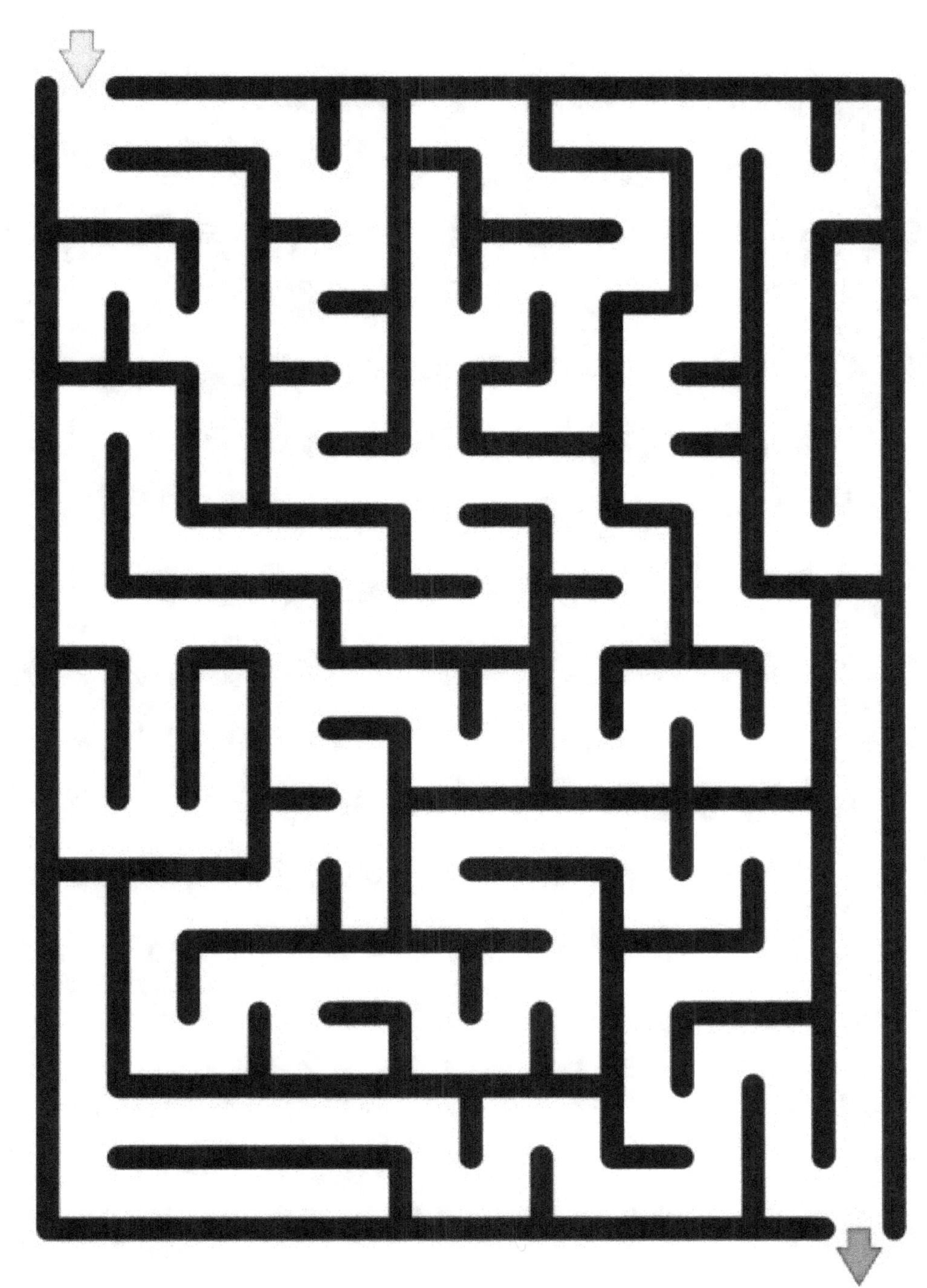

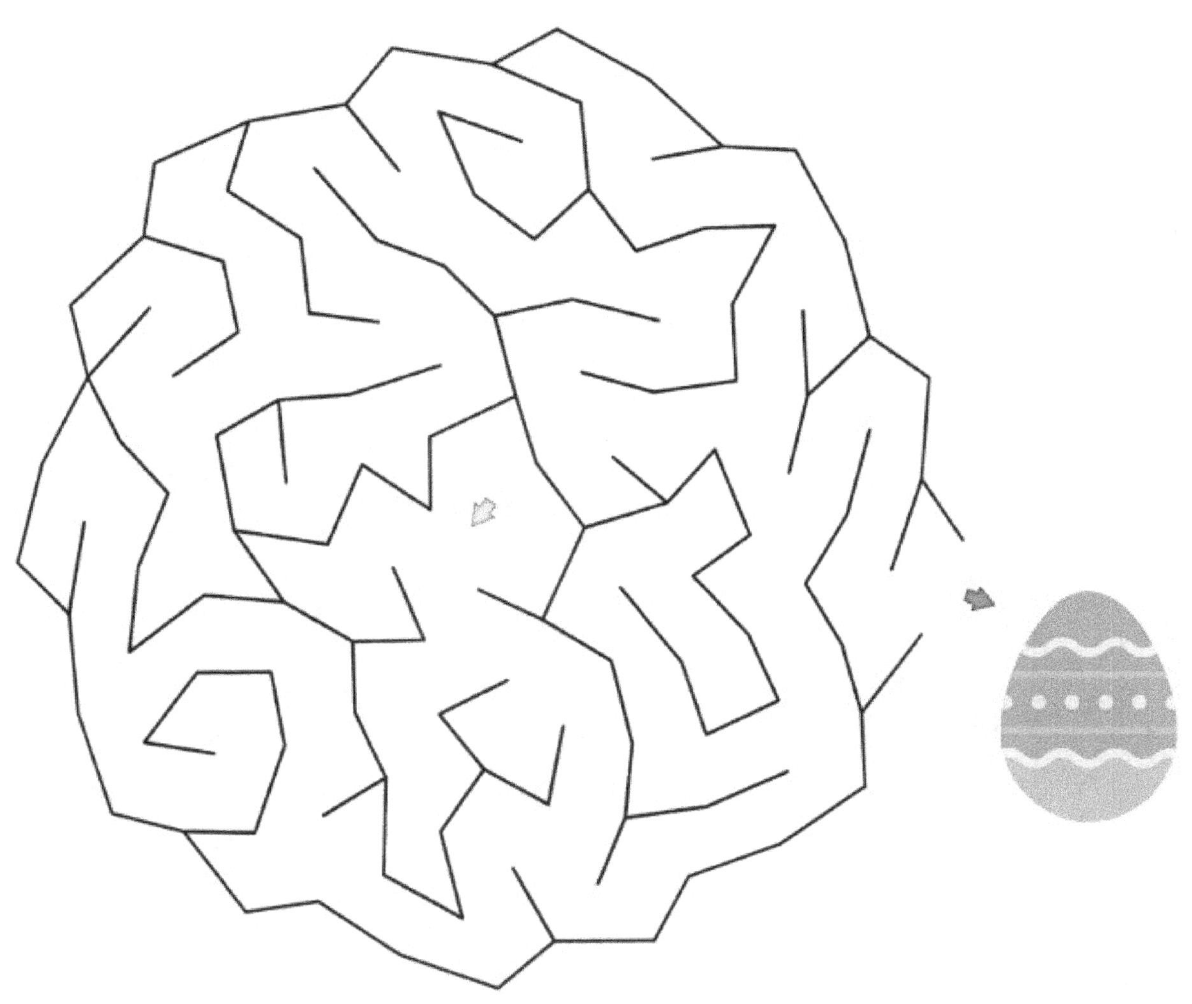

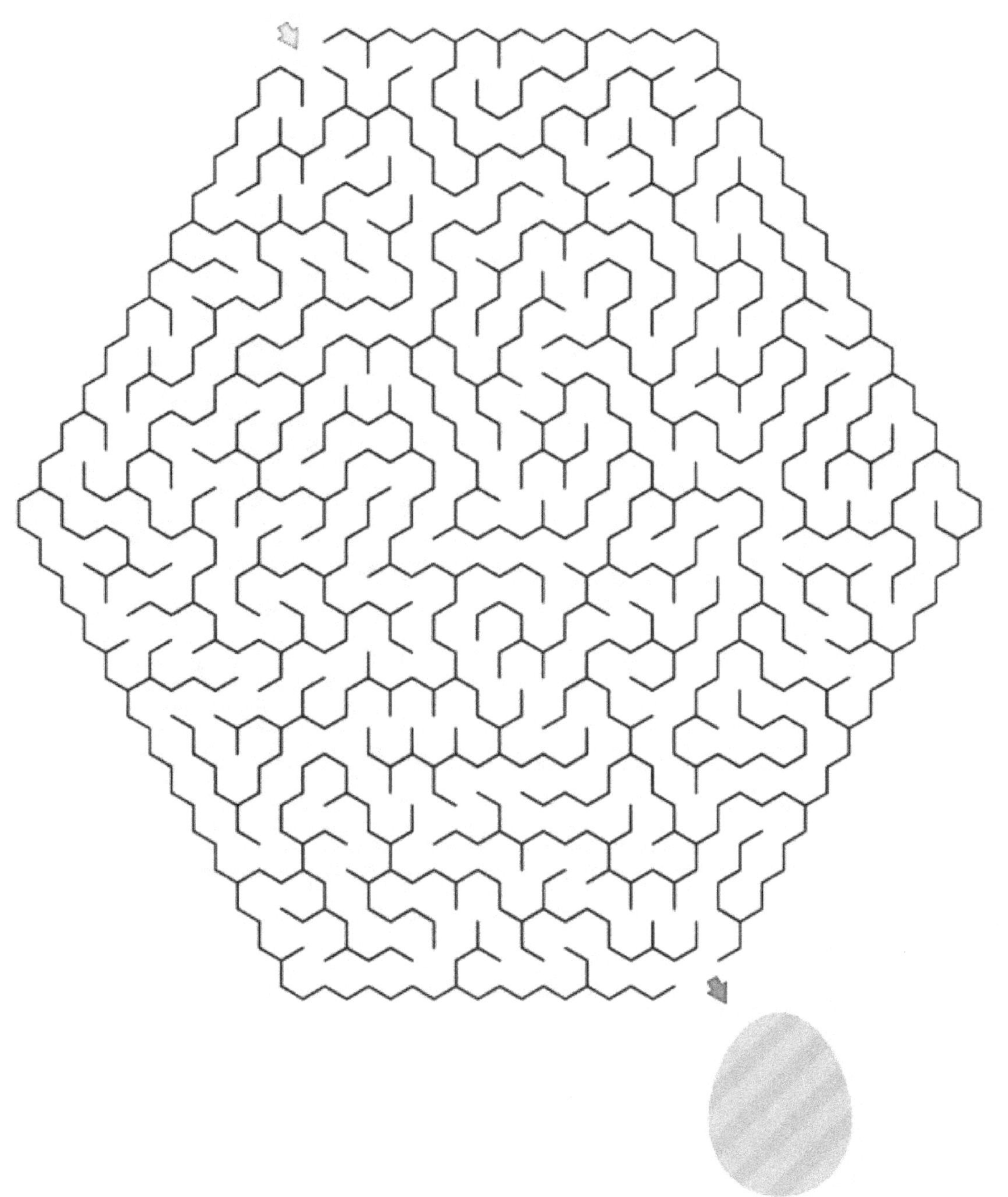

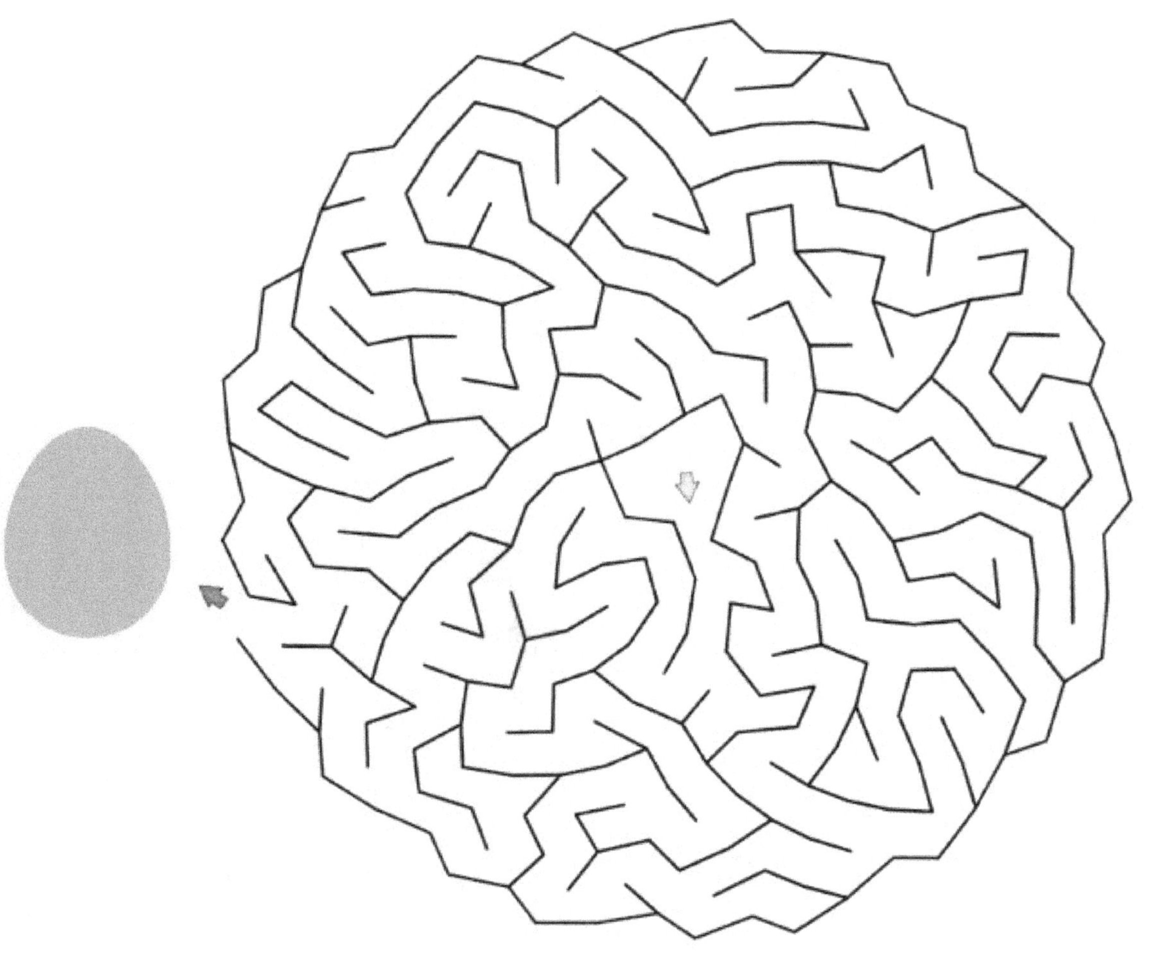